SELF-DISCIPLINE

A 21 Day Step by Step Guide to Creating a Life Long Habit of Self-Discipline, Powerful Focus, and Extraordinary Productivity

© Copyright 2018 by –David Clark- All rights reserved.

This document is geared towards providing exact and reliable information regarding topic and issue covered. The publication is sold with the idea that the publisher is not required to render accounting, officially permitted, or otherwise, qualified services. If advice is necessary, legal or professional, a practiced individual in the profession should be ordered.

- From a Declaration of Principles which was accepted and approved equally by a Committee of the American Bar Association and a Committee of Publishers and Associations.

In no way is it legal to reproduce, duplicate, or transmit any part of this document in either electronic means or in printed format. Recording of this publication is strictly prohibited and any storage of this document is not allowed unless with written permission from the publisher. All rights reserved.

The information provided herein is stated to be truthful and consistent, in that any liability, in terms of inattention or otherwise, by any usage or abuse of any policies, processes, or directions contained within is the solitary and utter responsibility of the recipient reader. Under no circumstances will any legal responsibility or blame be held against the publisher for any reparation, damages, or monetary loss due to the information herein, either directly or indirectly.

Respective authors own all copyrights not held by the publisher.

The information herein is offered for informational purposes solely, and is universal as so. The presentation of the information is without contract or any type of guarantee assurance.

The trademarks that are used are without any consent, and the publication of the trademark is without permission or backing by the trademark owner. All trademarks and brands within this book are for clarifying purposes only and are the owned by the owners themselves, not affiliated with this document.

Table of Contents

Introduction 1

Week 1: Beginning Your Self-Discipline Journey 3

    Day 1: Decide When to Wake Up Every Morning.........................5

    Day 2: Start a Physical Fitness Routine..8

    Day 3: Meditate, Meditate, Meditate 11

    Day 4: Cut Out Your Bad Habits..14

    Day 5: Learn to Reward Yourself the Right Way 17

    Day 6: Identify and Eliminate Time Wasters 20

    Day 7: Ask Yourself the Tough Questions.....................................23

Week 2: Setting Laser Sharp Focus on Your Future......................27

    Day 1: Create Long Term Goals with Short Term Actions 29

    Day 2: Where do You Want to Be in a Year? Five Years? Ten Years?....32

    Day 3: Figure Out What Type of Systems Work for You 40

    Day 4: Identifying Wants vs. Needs..43

    Day 5: Orient towards Long Term vs. Short Term Rewards 46

    Day 6: Surround Yourself with Focused People 48

Day 7: Decide What Actually Matters 51

Week 3: Productivity Hacks for Lifelong Success 53

Day 1: The Highlighter Conundrum 54

Day 2: Are You Productive or Just Busy? 57

Day 3: Set Measurable Daily, Weekly, and Monthly Goals 60

Day 4: Watch Out for Crabs in the Bucket 63

Day 5: Falling into the Complacency Trap 66

Day 6: Take Control of Your Work Environment 68

Day 7: Being Your Own Boss 71

Conclusion 73

INTRODUCTION

Congratulations on getting a copy of *Self-Discipline: A 21 Day Step by Step Guide to Creating a Life Long Habit of Self-Discipline, Powerful Focus, and Extraordinary Productivity.*

The following chapters will discuss how to truly live a life filled with focus, productivity, and self-discipline. These attributes are the most important things for someone who wants to live an exceptional and accomplished life, and the tips here are a 21-day step-by-step guide to lead you on your journey to becoming that person you always knew you could be.

There are plenty of books on this subject on the market, thanks again for choosing this one! Every effort was made to ensure it is full of as much useful information as possible, please enjoy!

WEEK 1:

BEGINNING YOUR SELF-DISCIPLINE JOURNEY

Day 1: Decide When to Wake Up Every Morning

How you start the day is usually an indication of how the rest of your day is going pan out. This is true for several reasons, the first and most important one being that the ability to get up at a reasonable hour and stick to a routine is an indication of a person who is disciplined and well organized.

If you have the willpower to wake up on time to make a solid breakfast and enjoy a morning routine, you have the mental strength and fortitude to power through the day with energy to spare. Additionally, getting up early allows you to get a solid amount of vitamin D, eat well, and mentally prepare for the day in a way that rolling out of bed after pressing snooze 12 times and being stressed out doesn't.

If you aren't already waking up at least an hour before you get started, you are operating about 55% less efficiently than you would be otherwise. Luckily, with a little discipline and patience, the tactics described below will get you waking up when you should and developing the self-discipline you need to take on the world.

Go to bed whenever you want, but wake up at the same time every day. There's no point forcing yourself to go to bed at 10:00 p.m. if you're used to falling asleep at 2:00 a.m. You'll just spend hours tossing and turning, and associate the bed with anxiety. What will work is setting an alarm for, say, 7:00 a.m. and getting up no matter how tired you are. It will be hard at first, but your body will get the picture that you're the boss, this is when you're getting up, and it will start to get tired at the right time.

Eat your meals at the same time every day. You can reprogram your body clock by doing this consistently every day. If you train yourself to know that breakfast is at 8:00 a.m., you'll wake up hungry in time to eat it. Similarly, if your body expects dinner at 7:00 p.m. and knows you go to bed four hours after dinner, it'll automatically start to get hungry and tired around those times.

Limit your caffeine intake. If you're drinking five cups of coffee throughout the day to compensate for being tired, you're in a dangerous cycle that will only get worse unless you cut down on the amount of coffee that you consume. Stop all caffeine 10 hours before bedtime, so if you're aiming at sleeping every night by 11:00 p.m., your last cup of coffee is at 1:00 p.m. It'll be tough for a few days, but you'll notice the benefits later.

Get sun first thing in the morning. A lot of what causes sleep disturbances in the modern world is that artificial lights are messing with the body's natural circadian rhythms. If you step outside first thing in the morning, no matter how badly you slept, you will feel more awake. Make this a habit, and get some sun on your face throughout the day. Combine this with limiting light exposure after sundown and you will find a marked improvement in your natural cycle.

Develop a bedtime routine. Having a wind-down routine is crucial if you're going to take control of your sleep habits and your life. I suggest turning off all electronics an hour before bed time, at a minimum. Other things you can do include taking a hot shower or bath, reading a book by a natural light like a candle, yoga, or something else to wind you down for the day. You can condition yourself through operant conditioning to associate these things with bedtime, and fall asleep much faster.

Day 2: Start a Physical Fitness Routine

Behind every successful person and entrepreneur is a physical fitness routine. The benefits of getting into physical fitness are huge, ranging from increased production of important chemicals in the brain, to developing general discipline and improved sleep. I have researched hundreds of CEOs and entrepreneurs, who all in some way credit their success to their efforts in the gym or other forms of regular workout.

There are a hundred different excuses you probably have for not being active, but all of them are simply a product of you either lying to yourself, or not believing in yourself. It takes twenty minutes a day to take a walk after dinner. Exercise videos are free on YouTube. Pajamas make good exercise clothes.

Think about this: how much time do you spend every day on things like Twitter or watching TV? Honestly, you could turn some of your TV time into workout time or do both together. Just doing a few sit-ups or squats while your dinner is cooking or watching an episode of a show will get you started into a routine. If you honestly believe you don't have time to do any fitness at all, take a long, hard look at your schedule. Three hours a night browsing Facebook is not an excuse to not go for an after-dinner walk.

That being said, it's important to start small and commit to a fitness regimen that you'll actually keep to and that is doable. There's a pretty common phenomenon where you go to the gym and feel amazing, promising yourself that you'll go every single day. A few days later, you skip one and instantly think,

"Oh well. I missed one day, I broke my promise, why bother trying again?"

Then you decide to completely stop going. This is counterproductive. It's much better to start small, with maybe one twenty-minute jog per week. You might read this and think, why bother? One jog a week isn't going to improve anything.

On the contrary, it will. Getting into the routine of moving is much better than not starting at all, and you can always increase your activity level later, once you've realized you can stick to a schedule.

I cannot emphasize the importance of setting a routine and starting small enough. There is going to come a time when you just don't feel like working out. Do it anyway. Even if all you manage to do is lace up your sneakers and do one sit-up, that's more than you would have done otherwise. Additionally, the odds are good that once you've done that one sit-up, you'll feel motivated to do more.

Go for a short ten-minute walk in the mornings. This is probably the easiest way to get started. Small morning walks get you moving at the beginning of the day, providing your body with much needed fresh air and sunshine.

Squat while brushing your teeth. Incorporating physical activity into everyday tasks like brushing your teeth is shockingly easy and effective. Anything you do many times a day, like browse the internet, watch Netflix, or type at a computer, you can also use this routine to do something like pushups, squats, or walking during it.

Go to the gym once a week, even if you just read a magazine. This is an amazing piece of advice by the great Terry Crews. It's important to build the habit of just going to the gym, even if you don't workout. Eventually, you'll associate being at the gym with feeling good and look forward to going.

Don't be afraid to switch it up. If you decide to run twice a week, and get bored after a few weeks, it makes perfect sense to switch to rock climbing or Zumba. Anything that gets you moving and keeps your attention is a good idea.

Keep yourself accountable with a workout partner. If somebody else is depending on you to show up to the gym, you're much more likely to follow through and actually go. It's harder to skip when you have a person counting on you to be there and workout with them.

Day 3: Meditate, Meditate, Meditate

"You should sit in meditation for twenty minutes every day - unless you're too busy. Then you should sit for an hour." -Zen proverb

Additionally, meditation has been shown to be one of the best ways of relieving stress. In this fast-paced world, the people who find success are the ones who are able to remain calm in the face of any or all obstacles and who can focus past the pressures of everyday life. Those people get their training on blood pressure control and calmness through daily meditation, often practiced in the morning before starting their workday. Below are two examples of meditations you can do, and a list of a few free meditation apps to get you started.

Morning meditation 1: As soon as you get out of bed in the morning, sit on the ground by your bed and close your eyes. Sit with your knees folded and hands on top of your knees. Spend ten minutes with your mind completely blank, focusing on nothing but your breath. Your breathing pattern will be this: breathe in for a count of 4, hold for a count of 4, breathe out for 7, and hold for 4. This breathing pattern has been scientifically shown to reduce stress and bring about a sense of calm. Be sure to set a timer so you aren't worried about the time while meditating.

Morning meditation 2: Just after waking, lie on the floor on your back. Your palms should be facing up, and you should be taking up as much space as possible. Set a timer to go off on your phone after fifteen minutes and put your phone aside. Picture yourself sitting in front of a cardboard box, in front of a fire, with a pile of paper in front of you. On each piece of paper, imagine a worry or concern that you have. Fold those pieces of paper up and place them in the box. Afterwards, place that box into the fire and watch all of the concerns go up in smoke; you will feel lighter and more focused.

Free Meditation Apps

Calm. This app has a range of guided meditations of various lengths, with some being as short as two or three minutes and others going up to 25 minutes. It's available for free on both iOS and Android with great reviews.

The Mindfulness App. This isn't just a meditation app; it actually gives you a small alert when it's time to meditate. You can also set the app's GPS to tell you to meditate when you get to a certain location, and program it to remind you during various times of the day to take a time out to meditate.

Inscape. One of the best features of Inscape is its five-day series introduction to meditation, which will help reduce your mental load and stress immediately. You can choose from a lot of meditations which will do things like help you sleep, breathe deeply, and wake up focused.

Pranayama. If you're a fan of breath control and learning deep breathing exercises, this app is for you. Pranayama takes you through different ways of tracking and controlling your breath, from associating it with sounds to counting down and others. This is a skill you can use on your own daily when any stress pops up.

Simple Habit. This is a really good meditation app for someone with a crazy schedule and not a lot of time. You can pick from over 1,000 meditations that last just five minutes each, so you'll never be bored and will always have time for one. This also includes a reminder, which you can set to tell you to meditate at the same time every day and there are longer meditations for when five minutes just isn't enough.

Day 4: Cut Out Your Bad Habits

This might seem like the most obvious advice in the world, but bear with me for a few minutes here. There are the obvious bad habits that are likely cutting into your life, such as smoking or drinking. These are things I think we can all universally agree are addictive and need to be cut out of the life of a disciplined and focused person.

Then, there are the more subtle and insidious bad habits you might have a hard time admitting you have. The most obvious example of this is too much time spent on social media. It's fine to spend an hour or so on Facebook catching up with your friends and family, but spending six hours a day liking pictures is valuable time that could have been spent on more productive things. It can be so easy to think 'oh I just spend a few minutes on it here and there,' but these add up fast, and the habit needs to change.

The ability to look in the mirror and honestly assess your strengths, weaknesses, and bad habits is essential to becoming the type of person you were always meant to be. It can be rough admitting how you really spend your day and what crutches you use to keep from achieving your goals, but it's time to face up to them.

Just like beginning a workout routine, it's important to start with small, attainable, concrete steps when you're quitting bad habits. For example, it's way easier to cut out two cigarettes a day from your smoking habit than it is to stop cold turkey. Similarly, it's easier to delete one social media app from your phone than to get rid of them all at once. If you try and stop everything destructive you're doing all at once, you have a higher chance of failure.

Another important factor when quitting bad habits is figuring out a good reason WHY you're stopping them. Giving good enough reasons to quit a bad habit is critically important. If the reasons are good and strong enough, they will automatically pull you into the direction of quitting.

Many people have tried to quit smoking for noble reasons like their family or their long-term health, but these are vague concepts and it's easy to do just one more, until the habit is formed again. If the reason for quitting smoking is important enough to you, such as setting a good example for your new born daughter, the process of letting go of that bad habit will be much easier.

The key thing to understand about breaking bad habits is that they're filling a void of some kind. You don't spend hours a day on YouTube or indulge in too much sugar for no reason; it's serving some kind of need in you. Whether your bad habit is taking up time, money, or you just have an addictive personality, you need to have something on hand to replace it with, once you quit the bad habit.

While the new habit needs to be better for you than what you're quitting, it must also be pleasurable in some way, or it won't work.

One example I know is a man who quit drinking and filled that time with video games. It's not ideal to spend hours a day playing Xbox, but it did keep him from drinking into oblivion every night. You can keep replacing bad habits with better and better ones until you have found something to enrich your life and improve your discipline.

Day 5: Learn to Reward Yourself the Right Way

If you attended high school science classes, you are probably familiar with Pavlov and his dogs. If you aren't or have forgotten that lesson, let's do a basic recap here. Pavlov was a behavioral scientist who was studying the effect of what's called 'operant conditioning' on animals. He trained his dogs to associate the sound of a bell with receiving a treat, and eventually they salivated in anticipation every time they heard that bell sound. The dogs had come to associate hearing a bell with reward, and their bodies prepared them for it.

What does this mean for you? After all, you're not a dog, and are capable of higher thoughts and understanding. Why is this relevant?

Being a self-aware and intelligent person does not mean that you are no longer susceptible to basic animal instincts and unconscious associations. What it does mean is that with a little creativity and discipline, you can use these parts of your nature to train yourself into being a more disciplined person. Instead of salivating to the sound of a bell, you'll teach yourself that working hard and being focused provide much stronger, better rewards than laziness and procrastination.

Keep in mind, the rewards that you train yourself to be disciplined with, need to enhance you as a focused person and an accomplished individual. Here are a few easy traps to fall in:

Giving yourself a reward that isn't enough of a motivator. If you're trying to condition yourself to focus on your work and not browse social media, a few sticks of celery for an hour of concentration is not going to be a strong enough end game.

Giving yourself a reward too late. An important factor in operant conditioning is timing. By giving yourself the reward hours or days after the desired behavior, you've lost the unconscious association. Ideally, you would get your reward just seconds after your accomplishments.

Giving yourself a reward that's counterproductive. Let's say you're trying to get up early every morning. It wouldn't make sense to reward yourself for getting out of bed by getting right back in for eight minutes of reward sleep. The reward must make sense.

Giving yourself a reward in advance. This is a really, really easy trap to fall into. It's tempting to give yourself the reward and promise yourself you'll do what you said, but it doesn't work. You need to reward yourself in the future, after a task is completed, so that the anticipation and excitement from knowing what you will receive pulls you forward trough completing that very task.

If you do it right, rewarding yourself is one of the most powerful basic psychological principles to enact meaningful change, and make yourself a disciplined person.

Make the reward something you don't get in everyday life. If you choose a pack of Twizzlers as your reward, but you already eat a lot of candy in everyday life, it's not going to have the same impact. If the reward is special, it's a lot more motivating.

Give someone else the power to give you the reward. If the reward you've chosen is tempting, it can be easy to backslide into the bad habits I've listed above. Giving the power to distribute the reward to someone else means that it's impossible for you to cheat and take it when you haven't earned it.

Size the reward to the accomplishment. Large scale accomplishments like finishing a huge work project early or losing fifty pounds deserve large rewards. Smaller accomplishments should be celebrated but cutting out one soda a day probably doesn't deserve an entire day off work.

Slowly decrease the reward with each instance of behavior. The idea behind motivating behavior through rewards is to eventually associate the behavior itself with pleasure, taking the need for the reward itself out of the equation. Slowly phase out the reward incentive until the new behavior is just a habit, and not something exceptional you have to reward yourself for each time.

Day 6: Identify and Eliminate Time Wasters

I'll keep the introduction brief: as there are several other things you're probably wasting your time with that are keeping you from being a disciplined person. Here are the biggest things to slowly phase out, if not entirely eliminate from your daily life.

Social media: There are a million different social media apps in the world, and they are all so easy to get lost in. You can get sucked into the vortex of Snapchat, Twitter, Facebook, LinkedIn, Instagram, Pinterest, Tumblr, and all of the others, without realizing you've wasted countless hours.

You should pick a MAXIMUM of two apps you'll keep, and spend no more than a half hour a day on those apps. The time you'll save and the discipline you'll gain is invaluable.

TV/Netflix: Have you head of the term 'binge watching'? With online streaming video, your favorite TV shows and movies are available instantly. That combined with the 'just one more episode' trap means that you're probably spending hours of your life watching TV.

Have you ever actually sat and added up all the time you spend watching content others created? Have you ever blown off work to watch an episode of something that you could actually just watch at any time? If you're not careful, it can go from a simple time waster to an actual full-blown addiction. Keep the time spend on watching TV or movies per day at a minimum and focus your attention on working on things that will actually improve your quality of life long-term.

Busy work: While this is not always entirely in your control, it's something to look out for. It's easy to do many small, unimportant things that feel like you're being really productive, when you're actually undisciplined and using those tasks as a way to avoid the hard work that is truly necessary to do. If you spend hours every day checking your email or reorganizing your office when there is a crucial phone call you have to make, you're not being disciplined or productive.

Outrageous favors: Disciplined people have one of the key attributes of success: the ability to say no. Everyone wants to feel liked, and it can often feel like you're being rude or a jerk when you turn someone down for something they need. Get into the habit of saying no to things you don't have time for, don't want to do, or that the person asking you could do for themselves will set you on a path of discipline and success. After all, you can't really build discipline and good habits that serve your life and priorities, if you're always putting other people before yourself.

Web browsing: Similar to social media, browsing the web can suck hours out of your day and motivation from your head without you realizing it. However, it can also lure you into the busy work trap, where you endlessly read blogs and articles about a course of action or task you need to accomplish without ever taking action yourself. Unless your web browsing serves a purpose that is both important and immediate or you've gotten everything crucial done for that day, put the mouse down and walk away from the humor web site.

Video games: Video games can be an especially insidious time waster because they can give you a false sense of accomplishment. Spending hours grinding away at a video game and beating a difficult level can feel really good and release those pleasure chemicals in the brain, similar to completing something in the real world. However, it's important to remember that in the long run, anything you've accomplished in a game isn't real and doesn't actually improve you as a person or help your discipline. Find satisfaction from solving and completing real tangible life problems. The sense of accomplishment and self-discipline you will receive will be far greater.

Day 7: Ask Yourself the Tough Questions

What are my strengths?

The true essence of developing self-discipline involves knowing yourself fully and intimately. It is tempting to look at the social media pages of entrepreneurs like Gary Vee and say to yourself, I can do that! I can work 14 hours a day! Let's grind!

It doesn't work that way for the vast majority of people.

If you try to be a second-rate Gary Vee or Ramit Sethi, then that's all you'll ever be. Every great leader and disciplined entrepreneur got there by figuring out what they're actually good at and capitalizing on their own strengths. You might have a hard time working with computers, but be a clever salesman. Find out what you're good at, work relentlessly with that, and figure out ways to compensate for the rest.

What are my weaknesses?

Similar to needing to truly understand your strengths, it's important to laser in and figure out your weaknesses. This isn't nearly as much fun as figuring out what you're good at, but is probably ten times more important because it will tell you where you can improve yourself.

While self-reflection is a plus, this is one area I recommend finding someone around you who you trust who will be honest with you, and ask them to tell you your weaknesses. It may take a bit of probing to get an honest answer, as most people are nice and won't want to hurt your feelings. Press them until they actually give you something concrete and truthful that you can improve upon, take their advice with a smile and without getting defensive, and set out on your course of self-improvement.

What's really stopping me?

Take a long, hard look at your life and yourself. You probably already know on an intellectual level where you want to be in life and what you need to do for success and to be a disciplined person. Why haven't you done so yet? Are you afraid of failure? Do you worry about what everyone else is going to say? Have you simply gotten too comfortable? Answer these questions for yourself, then think about them and answer them again more honestly. Keep digging until it actually feels terrifying and uncomfortable. After all, it's said that life begins where your comfort zone ends and that's also true of discipline and self-improvement.

How can I get my time back?

A large part of this is going to come down to the time wasters we discussed previously, such as social media, Netflix, and busy work. Eliminating those is a start, but let's dig deeply into where your time is going and how you can get it back under your control, which leads to getting your life under control.

Some of this is going to be tough, as time consuming people and habits can become deeply enmeshed in your idea of who you are. You may feel like you're being a horrible person for cutting off a relationship with someone who demands a lot of your time without giving anything in return, but you have every right to do so. You can't sink yourself to keep someone else from drowning. Take your time back.

Who am I blaming besides myself?

The harsh truth is that if you aren't disciplined, it's completely on you. If you ever hope to be a disciplined and successful person you can't blame any of those people around you for the state your life is in right now. Your parents may not have taught you about money, your friends may take your time, your boss may not have promoted you, but this doesn't mean you can't take care of those things by and for yourself. Be accountable. Teach yourself how to manage money. Get rid of that friendship. Shop around for better job offers and use those as leverage with your boss. Once you accept that you're responsible for your own success and / or failure, you will be liberated from relying on things you can't control for success and happiness.

WEEK 2:

SETTING LASER SHARP FOCUS ON YOUR FUTURE

Day 1: Create Long Term Goals with Short Term Actions

Once you've built the discipline to go after any goal or task that comes your way, it's time to focus on the goals you will be using that discipline to really go for. There are any number of goals you can choose to focus on, ranging from financial goals to personal fitness goals, and everything in between.

There is a trap you need to avoid falling into, however, and that is setting yourself vague goals that sound good, but are not clearly defined. Let's take personal fitness for an example.

Bad goal: I want to get in shape.

Good goal: I want to lose two pounds a week by going to the gym for an hour every Monday, Wednesday, and Friday.

Do you see why the good goal works and the bad goal doesn't? Wanting to 'get in shape' is like wanting to 'get rich.' It can mean almost anything. If you set a concrete goal that includes specific actions you will take to achieve it, that's considered a good goal to strive for. Here are a few other guidelines to keep in mind when setting your measurable long-term goals that contain short term, actionable items within them.

Don't set goals that are too hard or too easy. The reason why you shouldn't set goals that are too hard is obvious. After all, if your goal is to make a million dollars in a week and you haven't set up the infrastructure to do so, you'll feel disappointed when you inevitably fail. For a goal to be worthwhile, it must be achievable. That being said don't let yourself get away with setting goals that are too easy either, like 'drink one less can of coke per month.' That's so basic it's not worth writing down. A goal should measurably change your life and provide more satisfaction than that. You're better than that. Aim higher.

Don't set goals that you just 'think' you should aim for. In everyone's life, there are things they are expected to do and things that they actually truly want to do which light a fire inside them. Let's say you're a college student! If your parents are dying for you to become a lawyer, you might have set the goal of getting into law school. However, if what you actually want is to be a business owner, you're setting yourself up for misery even if you do reach this goal. Pick a goal that truly makes you excited and keen to jump out of bed to get to work in the morning, even if it isn't what you're expected to do. After all you only have one life, why not live it the way you want to?

Set measurable, specific goals. Just like in the example above, a goal should not only be specific it should be quantifiable measurable. If we look at a common goal, a lot of people want to get rich. Well, what does that actually mean? Do you want to have a million dollars in your bank account by the time you turn a certain age? Do you want to be able to afford a certain car or house? Do you want an investment portfolio that generates a $40,000.00 income per month? Figure out not just that you want money, but what you want that money to do for you. If you can set a goal with an actual number, you can break it down into pieces and start making a plan. It's much simpler to set up a drop shipping business that generates $7,000.00 per month of passive income than it is to 'get rich.'

Set realistic goals. A goal has to be realistic to work. This doesn't mean that you shouldn't expect a lot from yourself and aim high, but it does mean you need to actually be able to achieve what you're going for. Don't set your newfound laser focus on something that you know isn't possible to ensure you don't feel bad when you fail. Don't aim for failure. Taking a risk on something that MIGHT fail is scary, but focusing all your time and energy on something that WILL fail because it's safe, is a waste of your life.

Day 2: Where do You Want to Be in a Year? Five Years? Ten Years?

I'd like to get even more specific. If you want to be a more focused person, that's great, but focus only improves your life when you have a good clear idea of where it is you want to end up and the route you need to take to get there. You should make up a chart or path with one-year, five-year, and ten-year fitness, financial, and just for fun milestones and goals. Underneath those goals will be three steps you'll take to achieve each one. Attached here is an example, as well as a blank roadmap for you to use when making your own focused goal roadmap!

EXAMPLE ROADMAP

<u>One year:</u>

Fitness: I will be able to run a 5k race in under 45 minutes without stopping or walking.

> Step 1: Two runs in the park per week using the free Couch to 5k app.
>
> Step 2: Replace the soda I drink at work with water.
>
> Step 3: Weight lifting twice per week, focusing on leg muscles and core strength.

Financial: I will be able to pay off the $1,000.00 balance on my credit card.

> Step 1: Instead of buying Starbucks every morning, put that money into a savings account.
>
> Step 2: Go to one less restaurant meal per month.
>
> Step 3: Pick up a part time job as a babysitter, waitress, or bartender one Saturday or Sunday evening each week.

Just for fun: Be able to cook an entire Thanksgiving meal on my own.

> Step 1: Learn how to make a pie from scratch.
>
> Step 2: Practice using a meat thermometer.
>
> Step 3: Divide the meal into sections and make one each week leading up to Thanksgiving as a dry run.

Five years:

Fitness: Do eight pull-ups in a row without stopping.

> Step 1: Increase my daily protein intake to 125 grams through tofu, fish, and healthy veggies.

Step 2: Increase all upper body training to four times a week including 5 x 5 pushups, assisted pull-ups, dips, curls, rows, bench presses, and overhead presses.

Step 3: allocate at least one rest day between these workouts.

Financial: Increase my income by $5,000.00 per year.

Step 1: Start a sideline business, say freelance writing, to earn an extra $500.00 per month.

Step 2: Get together my past work performance and sit down with the boss to discuss a raise.

Step 3: Interview for one job a week which would include a pay increase.

Just for fun: Play 'Pressure' by Paramore on the acoustic guitar.

Step 1: Purchase an appropriately sized guitar.

Step 2: Research guitar lessons and take lessons with an instructor once a week.

Step 3: Practice on my own for twenty minutes twice a week.

Ten years:

Fitness: Run a full marathon.

Step 1: Go on 45 minutes runs four times a week.

Step 2: Ensure to get 10 hours of sleep each night.

Step 3: Run one half marathon distance per week, in the two months leading up to the big race.

Financial: Have a side business that brings in $10,000.00 per month in passive income.

Step 1: Research product ideas that cost at least $100.00 in a hobby or group I am involved in.

Step 2: Invest in a simple business page and targeted advertising to test the validity of the idea.

Step 3: Hire an assistant from Brickwork or Tasks Everyday to run the day to day operations of said idea.

Just for fun: Have a ten-minute conversation in Japanese with a native speaker.

Step 1: Purchase the Rosetta Stone Japanese language learning kit. Use it three times a week for 30 minutes.

Step 2: Attend any Japanese meet up groups in the area.

Step 3: Choose a favorite book and read the entire Japanese translation.

YOUR ROADMAP – FILL THIS OUT TODAY

One year:

Fitness:

Step 1:

Step 2:

Step 3:

Financial:

Step 1:

Step 2:

Step 3:

Just for fun:

Step 1:

Step 2:

Step 3:

Five years:

Fitness:

Step 1:

Step 2:

Step 3:

Financial:

Step 1:

Step 2:

Step 3:

Just for fun:

Step 1:

Step 2:

Step 3:

Ten years:

Fitness:

Step 1:

Step 2:

Step 3:

Financial:

Step 1:

Step 2:

Step 3:

Just for fun:

Step 1:

Step 2:

Step 3:

Day 3: Figure Out What Type of Systems Work for You

The key to being focused and productive is to be an organized person. Organized people have great systems in place to handle all the small things that come up. These are my recommendations for the most important categories in your life, so you never miss anything and lose focus trying to track it down again.

Organizing notes: The only app that matters for organizing your notes is called Evernote. This is an absolutely amazing little app which keeps all your notes, sketches, and information in one place. You can do amazing things like take pictures of business cards, and Evernote will translate it into text which is searchable for you later. The search function is truly Evernote's shining star, you can just snap pictures of all the physical pieces of paper you're storing in your desk and keep it all in one easy to manage place.

Managing workflow: There are a lot of good systems out there for managing workflow, but I find that the most elegant and simple is Asana. It's a free project management app, which lets you divide tasks into individual projects and sub tasks. It doesn't have all the bells and whistles of a lot of project management and workflow apps might offer, but that's what I like about it. You can divide tasks into easily moveable and manageable units, assign different ones to different people or companies, and just keep on top of everything you have to do, without going crazy.

Calendar: I know this is counterintuitive, but I'm a fan of a good old-fashioned paper planner or desk calendar. The act of putting pen to paper will help imprint your To Dos in your memory, and it not being electronic means you don't lose everything with a glitch. Additionally, the limited space forces you to only add important things, as it's easy to add ten thousand to dos on an app without space limits. You should of course back up pictures of your calendar pages on Evernote but a paper planner cannot be beaten.

Communication systems: Hands down, the best way to keep yourself and any team organized is with an app called Teamwork. You've probably heard of this app if you've spent any time working remotely, and there is a pretty strong reason why it's number one in its arena. You can keep all your communication in one place, not have to rely on endless email strings to plan things, create different private and public channels depending on who you're talking to, the list is truly endless. If you need something that works for a team, Teamwork is the best and most aptly named service.

Keeping out distractions: If you're going to eliminate distractions, the first thing to do is delete all of the social media apps off your phone and tablet. There is nothing that will ruin your concentration faster than going to check endless notifications. Next, set your email to only actually deliver email three or four times a day so you aren't constantly bombarded and interrupted by new notifications. Finally, for when you really need to get things done, there are a huge number of websites and apps that will block time wasting sites for however long you need to. Shop around and find your favorite!

Tracking long term goals: Once again, I recommend going low tech on this one. Earlier, I listed a worksheet that you can print on paper and fill out outlining long term goals for one, five, and ten years. Print out a few copies of that on paper and put them by your bedroom mirror, calendar, desk, and anyplace else you need inspiration. The satisfaction you'll feel crossing out those milestones and goals with actual pen is way better than just deleting them off something electronic. Trust me.

Day 4: Identifying Wants vs. Needs

If you are really going to put your laser focus on something, it has to be something that you NEED. If whatever you're going for doesn't light a fire in your soul, and make you desire it above all else, it's going to be hard to focus when things get rough. Just like the goal map we outlined before, let's go through a few differences of financial, interpersonal, and physical things you might want vs. need. Take care to look at the mindset of the two contrasting points of view and see which one you relate to more.

Financial

Want: I think it would be kind of nice to be rich someday, I guess. I mean my job is OK but I find myself still drowning in a lot of student loan debt. Every day I go to work and I feel myself die a little inside and I really want to make a change. I guess I'll send out resumes or finally start that business, tomorrow though, I want to finish that last level of Borderlands tonight and I think Jeopardy is on. I'm too tired, maybe I'll do it tomorrow, but I am going to do it.

Need: I know that I deserve a better and more financially secure life than I've got right now, and I'll do whatever it takes to make that happen. I'll spend two hours sending out resumes to recruiters and applying for jobs, then another hour tonight setting up a website for that business idea I've always had. The time to take action is right now and I won't be able to sleep tonight unless I know I've made real progress towards an extra $5,000.00 per month to put towards my future and that of my family.

Interpersonal

Want: I've been feeling really lonely lately, it would be nice to have some more friends to go out with. I'll like some friends' pictures on Facebook, maybe that will make them take notice of me and invite me out. I wish I could invite people over, but I don't even know what I'd have them do. Oh, I got invited to a party, but I really don't know if I'll know everyone there, I'll click no and go to the next one that I'm invited to. There's always tomorrow and anyway the Apprentice is on tonight.

Need: I'm going to make a list of the ten people who I enjoy spending time with the most, and reach out to one of them per day, just to say hello and find out how they're doing. I've started volunteering at the animal shelter and have joined a kickball team in order to meet friends and dates who have the same interest, and I've made sure to attend every party I go to, even if I didn't necessarily want to at first. Social interaction is a higher priority to me than anything else right now, I can't keep going on as usual, while feeling miserably lonely like this.

Fitness

Want: That's weird, all of my jeans are starting to get a little bit tight. I'm afraid to weigh myself because I know it'll have jumped up by at least five or ten pounds. Oh wow, I'm twenty pounds higher than I thought, I really should lose some weight. I'll start eating healthier after this next candy bar. After this next meal. After my nephew's birthday party. I'll go to the gym tomorrow, it's too rainy outside. I'm too tired to workout. I should lose the weight and I know that I'm going to start at some point soon. I want to get thin, and I will at some point, eventually.

Need: I've had enough of this; I want to fit back into the dress/suit I wore on my wedding day. I'm going to throw out all the junk food in my house, download a calorie counting app like My Fitness Pal, and commit to three gym days a week. Even when it's raining or I'm tired, I'm going to work out those three days until I'm so tired I can't move. If I go over calories one day, I'll get right back on the horse the next day, until I meet my goal. I won't stop until I fit back into that outfit even if it means losing TV or video game time.

Day 5: Orient towards Long Term vs. Short Term Rewards

An easy trap is to fall into is wanting everything right now, right now, right now. There is a lot of truth in good things coming to those who wait, and that is no exception when it comes to rewards. It's a mistake to think of a reward just as a piece of chocolate or a favorite video game, those are easy things to get that feel good, but don't provide nearly as much long-term satisfaction. When you're deciding how to reward yourself, keep in mind that a lot of the time what you're working toward is a reward and you will value working harder to gain long term rewards much more than short term rewards you can buy at a store.

What kind of rewards you eventually start to orient towards will define you as a person eventually. If you believe that the only rewards are things which are time wasting and destructive, such as video games and soda, then that's how you're going to define pleasure and success. Train yourself to see the value in things you used to have to force yourself to do, such as going on a gorgeous run outside instead of in the gym. Learn how to truly enjoy something that is good for you and enriches you as a person, and what used to be something you had to reward yourself to do will become its own satisfying reward.

Gary Vee once asked his audience, "Are you willing to eat shit for a year in order to eat caviar for the rest of your life?" I think that's a really great question, and an important one to ask yourself when thinking about what's truly valuable and rewarding. If you can love the process, the grind, blocking everything else out that the people around you waste their lives on and hyper focus on building your empire, then I think you're one of the few who will actually reach the top. Let me tell you, the view is to die for.

Day 6: Surround Yourself with Focused People

There's a pretty famous expression that says, 'you are the sum of the five people you spend the most time with.' There's another similar expression that reads, 'if you want to know the character of a man, simply look at the company he keeps.' You cannot escape the influence of the people around you. If all of your friends are unhappy with their jobs and feel stuck in their lives, their complaining and attitude will very likely transfer over to you. If your friends are all overweight, it's likely all your interactions revolve around food and you all share similar attitudes towards it.

On the other hand, if your friends are motivated to better their lives that enthusiasm and infectious attitude will only make your life better. It can sound cold to say that you should spend a lot less time around people who make you feel stuck and depressed, after all, what if they need you? Isn't it mean to cut off a friendship just because that person isn't where you necessarily would want to be in life?

No. It isn't. You can't set yourself on fire just to keep someone else warm. There's no reason to be mean or cold about why you're suddenly not available to hang out with a friend who does nothing but complain, but make yourself less available to them. Your life and your own attitude and focus will thank you for this.

That being said, it's important to figure out who does inspire you and make sure to spend as much time around those people as possible. Surrounding yourself with friends who understand ambition, who care about their lives and prioritize being accomplished and focused people will make you so much better. There is just no way to replicate that kind of positivity, which will hopefully crowd out the negativity from people who see you improving and want to keep you down, to make yourself feel better.

Those positive influences don't have to be real life friends! They can be authors, bloggers, or influencers that you like, even if you haven't met them in person. You will get more out of spending two hours reading the biography or guide book of someone who has the focus and discipline you want, than you will spending two weeks with friends who only serve to drag you down and make you lesser than you can be.

You won't be able to feel the influence of these positive people if you don't get the people lowering you out of your sphere and life. The first thing to do is create a list of friends that you dread seeing, that you would never trade lives with, and who do nothing but complain. Make an effort to spend no more than one hour per month with these people, less if at all possible. It might sound extreme, but you will feel so much better for it.

There are two ways to get the toxic people out of your life: the slow fade and the nuclear. It's a lot easier to slowly grow apart from people, as most people are absorbed in their own lives and likely won't realize what it is that you're doing and why. You can simply stop being available for parties, reply late to messages, and all they will know is that you have drifted apart.

The nuclear option is for those who won't get the hint, or anyone who is so toxic and codependent your efforts to drift away only make them cling tighter. I know it's hard to say outright that you no longer want to be friends with someone, but it is so important for your focus, self-discipline, productivity, and growth. Whether you do it in a Facebook message or a phone call, all that matters is you bite that bullet sooner rather than later.

Day 7: Decide What Actually Matters

For all we've talked about focus this week, there's one key aspect of being a focused person we haven't covered: the realization that you can't have everything you want at the same time. It just isn't possible. For you to focus on your family, your physical fitness will have to slide. If you're really zeroing in on your financial situation, you're probably going to neglect your hobbies and fun time. Accepting this very basic truth is the final hurdle towards becoming focused and disciplined, before we move on to how you can become truly productive. Once you stop trying to go for everything at the same time, you're free to purse what truly matters.

One good way to figure out what it is you truly want, and therefore what you should be focusing on, is by imagining yourself at the age of 90, on your death bed. Will you regret most not having written your novel? Will you regret not spending time with your family? What scares you to your core when you think about whether you would regret not taking the opportunity to achieve that particular goal in your life? You'll know you have found the thing that the laser-like focus you've been honing should be targeted to, when you find what stops your heart at the thought of never actually getting to do or accomplishing it.

As soon as you know the one, two, or at the most three things you need to put all your focus into, it's time to forget the rest. We did a lot of the groundwork in week one by giving up bad habits and setting yourself up to be able to let go of things that don't matter. That was easy mode, though, and this is hard mode. The simple truth is that you cannot pursue opening a restaurant, getting your medical degree, and losing 75 pounds all at the same time. There are only so many hours in the day, and you need to spend some of them doing things like eating and sleeping and showering. Figure out which dream matters the most to you, and pursue that with a single mindedness that makes the old you quake with fear.

WEEK 3:

PRODUCTIVITY HACKS FOR LIFELONG SUCCESS

Day 1: The Highlighter Conundrum

The highlighter conundrum is a state of being where a student marking their textbook in order to prepare for an exam will end up not having any idea what actually matters for the test, so they end up just highlighting everything in different colors. This renders the highlighting useless, if everything is highlighted than frankly nothing is actually emphasized.

Productivity is a lot like that. If you try and be productive at everything all at the same time, you'll end up being productive at nothing. This is true for productivity, focus, and success alike, and it is very important to know the difference between simply appearing to be productive and actually being productive.

What productivity looks like: Answering several hundred emails per day for several hours a day. Accepting any and all work that is thrown your way and finishing it even, if it takes hours longer than you had planned on working. Getting everything done even if something is low priority and taking away from something else. Filing more papers and attending more meetings than anyone else in the office.

What productivity actually is: Knowing which things to work hard on and which things can sit on the back burner. Setting up systems so you only have to do repetitive tasks like answer emails and pay bills once a week. Spending an hour doing something the right way, so you don't have to spend four hours fixing your mistakes made when rushing a job. Prioritizing which meetings are important and which can be missed, to maximize efficiency.

What focus looks like: Taking direction from everyone and applying it to your work regardless of where it's coming from. Ignoring important last-minute work to plow through the project in front of you. Downing five cups of coffee and working at lightning speed. Working slowly to ensure everything is perfect without considering deadlines.

What focus actually is: Concentrating on your job at hand, despite a taxing work environment or distracting coworkers. Knowing yourself and when it's important to take breaks in order to not have to redo tasks. Getting enough sleep to maintain concentration. Getting it done right the first time, but being open to switching tasks and maintaining concentration, if priorities rapidly shift. Staying calm and maintaining perspective, even when there are fires to put out.

What success looks like: Having three luxury cars and a million-dollar house. Sending your kids to private school for their education. Going on four exotic vacations to interesting countries every year. Showing off new brand name clothes at your country club. Eating out at expensive restaurants with your coworkers every day. Never wearing the same outfit or pair of shoes twice. Having a wine cellar stocked with interesting and exotic wines. Going to clubs where the entry fee is $35.00 and drinks are at least $15.00 each. Taking a cab everywhere, instead of the bus. Living what most would call luxuriously.

What success actually is: Having enough money in your savings account to survive for a year if you lose your job. Maxing out your 401k and IRA to be sure you can retire comfortably. Being able to get a traffic ticket without it screwing up your budget for the entire month. Paying for cars and vacations in cash, not on credit. Living within a very comfortable means and building up for long term financial stability. An investment portfolio and retirement fund. Never being scared that your high-ticket items and expensive house are going to bankrupt you. True financial freedom and security always.

Day 2: Are You Productive or Just Busy?

As discussed above, being productive and looking productive are often two very different things. But what about being productive vs. feeling productive? After all, if you spend the day making several hundred cold sales calls that could be done much faster with a simple email or through a Facebook ad campaign, are you actually being productive?

Or are you just being busy?

Making yourself busy in the modern world is really easy. It can feel good to individually clear out hundreds of old junk emails, spend hours shopping around to find the lowest price flight, or applying to jobs you're over qualified for that you don't truly want. Those things keep you busy, but are you actually being productive?

No.

Being productive isn't just about literally getting anything or everything done. If that was the case, then a man who spends all day stacking pennies in a pile is a productive person. Someone who is genuinely, truly productive is getting things done in an efficient matter, but knows which things actually have to get done They are doing what needs all their focus and productive energy to make a tangible difference.

Often times, people use busy work as a way to avoid doing the work that is hard, scary, or difficult, but way more important. This is often seen in college students, who suddenly find themselves doing laundry and deep cleaning the refrigerator when finals are coming up. These students are technically getting stuff done, but are actually avoiding being productive, by staying busy at something else instead.

The same is true in your life. If you want to lose weight, this might look like spending hours researching protein shakes and nutrition macros rather than making that first visit to the gym. If you're trying to get promoted this could look like doing a lot of organizing of your desk, but not scheduling that meeting to ask your boss for a promotion or raise.

It's great to get a lot of stuff done, but the hard work that you're avoiding is where your productivity needs to be focused.

You can avoid getting sucked into this trap by taking the time to ask yourself a few times a day,

"Am I being productive, or am I just being busy?"

"Is what I'm doing important, or am I doing what I'm doing to avoid important work?"

This exercise won't work if you can't be honest with yourself about your habits and priorities.

You have to be willing to be uncomfortable, which is a necessary evil of looking at yourself in the mirror and telling yourself the truth about your life and your habits. It also helps to identify two or three main goals you want to accomplish every day when you make up that must all be important and difficult. This will get you in the habit of doing the tough things and not putting them off to answer emails and return unnecessary phone calls. If you are willing to face this truth and do the tough stuff anyway, you're on your way to a wonderful and productive life.

Day 3: Set Measurable Daily, Weekly, and Monthly Goals

While we have discussed setting one-year, five-year, and ten-year goals in a previous chapter, I want to touch on daily, weekly, and monthly goals you can aim for, to keep yourself productive and accountable in the short term as well. Setting these goals and evaluating them ensures that your productive energy is serving you well and keeping you not just busy, but truly on target with your best and most amazing laser focused, self-disciplined, and productive life.

Daily goals

1. This may seem obvious, but daily goals need to be something that actually can be accomplished in a single day. It's admirable to say that you're going to change your life by running ten miles or raise $10,000.00, but that's better as a longer-term goal.

2. You should have no more than three crucial, important daily goals that you want to accomplish. This is something great to focus on during your morning meditations, actually deciding what you want and need to get done that day. Write those goals down on a piece of paper and keep that with you, crossing them off as they are completed.

3. Don't ever go to sleep without getting those daily goals done. The tossing and turning will keep you up all night, and the lack of self-worth is pretty tough to sleep with. Even if you need to stay up an hour extra, that feeling of accomplishment makes for a much better night's rest afterwards.

Weekly goals

1. One weekly goal is a great amount to keep you productive and on your toes. This can be broken down into daily tasks to keep you on track, or you can pick one day a week dedicated to achieving these particular goals.

2. Put your weekly goal into your electronic or paper calendar! Having that written reminder of your need to accomplish it will keep you on mission. After all, you don't want a goal to be out of sight and so out of mind. You want it in front of your eyes and kept in mind, so that it actually gets done.

3. Just because you have a weekly goal does not mean you now have an excuse to create busy work to supposedly meet that goal. Every step you take towards it must be immediate, important, and ideally difficult. Otherwise you're just falling back into the busy trap, which is the worst place to be for someone like you who wants to be successful and focused and productive in everything they do.

Monthly goals

Ideally, you've planned out your one-year, five-year, and ten-year goals. The monthly milestones and goals you set should be stepping stones towards reaching those bigger things. It's fine to have monthly goals of their own accord, but wouldn't it be great if those were serving your long-term discipline, focus, and success? Having monthly stepping stones means you're being productive and working on these will make those long-term goals a piece of cake, until it's time to retire very, very, very early and richly.

Day 4: Watch Out for Crabs in the Bucket

Have you ever seen a bunch of crabs in a bucket? It's kind of amazing to watch. One of them will figure out the way out of the bucket and back to freedom, but the other crabs will all drag him back down, in an effort to get out themselves.

Have you gotten the obvious metaphor yet?

When you start to ramp up your life and truly tap into your own productivity and focus, there are going to be people around you who are just like those crabs. They want to pull you back down into the bucket. These people feel trapped and miserable, like they never have a chance to escape the bucket.

You leaving the bucket reminds them that they in fact do have a choice over their own lives and achievements, and that's something people who weren't smart enough to buy a copy of this book simply cannot face. Unless you want to become those people, you need to identify them and keep them away from you.

There are several signs that someone is a crab in disguise.

1. They are incredibly bitter whenever you show some sign of success. A person who you want to be around will be happy for you whenever you succeed at something. A crab is only able to focus on themselves and how bitter your success

makes them feel, and how it reminds them they didn't succeed or produce.

2. They constantly try to drag you down to their level. A crab can't bear to see someone do something they didn't or couldn't do, so they'll try and drag you back into their own comfort zone. Crabs will sabotage a work day by taking credit, will sabotage a diet by putting sweets everywhere, anything to stop them from facing their own failures.

3. Crabs can be easily identified by their reaction to your success and good news. If someone is happy for you and wants to know how you did it and to celebrate with you, that's a friend. If someone wants to tell you why that isn't impressive and why that's a bad thing and why you should stop trying, that's a crab.

Just as important as knowing how to identify crabs is knowing how to fight them.

1. Suddenly become deaf when a crab tries to tell you how to live your life. Their "advice" is never helpful and is always, always going to be self-serving. A good rule of thumb is to never take advice from someone that you wouldn't trade lives with, and that goes double for people who actively want to make your life worse.

2. Cut crabs out of your life completely. If someone in your life can't be happy that you're becoming more productive and successful, that isn't someone worth being around. We discussed ways to remove those who don't serve you from your life, and that's doubly important when dealing with crabs.

3. Keep your goals in mind. When others are telling you that you can't do something and trying to drag you down, it's time to double down on focus and productivity. Use the anger you feel as fuel to prove those who try and drag you back into the bucket are very wrong.

Day 5: Falling into the Complacency Trap

I want you to take a really long, hard look at your life. The chances are pretty good that you aren't actually miserable or desperate to change something. You more likely just have a nagging feeling that you SHOULD be doing something different, that you COULD be doing more, but that everything is just fine right now as it is. After all, you have a decent job that pays the bills, your life is going along OK, so why change things up?

The most terrifying thing imaginable isn't extreme unhappiness. That kind of unhappiness leads people to understand they must change to live a productive and fulfilling life. What you really should be worried about is getting stuck in a boring existence that's fine for right now. That kind of trap can take years to identify, and can be much harder to get out of than something objectively worse.

When you're comfortable but bored, you're in a dangerous zone of living an unexceptional and unproductive life. It's well documented that an object at rest stays at rest, and you don't want to be that resting object. If you've made it this far in the book, you must know on some level that there's more out there, that there is something better than looking at your life and not feeling much excitement. However, if you wake up every day not being excited to go into the office, go home and play video games, and repress all the dreams you've given up on because things are fine for now; chances are you've fallen into the complacency trap.

A great cure for the complacency trap is shocking change. It's time to start doing things that scare you. Purposely make yourself uncomfortable. If there's anything you've been putting off because it seems like too big a risk, if making a choice or starting a project feels like that moment before the big drop at the height of a roller coaster... that's what you should be doing. Don't let yourself become complacent and watch the years pass by with no real significance. You can either be the person on your death bed smiling at your adventures, or wistfully thinking of the life you could have fully lived.

Day 6: Take Control of Your Work Environment

We've talked a lot about theory and about mindset, but there's something practical that's unbelievable important for productivity – your work environment! Your environment has more of an effect on your productivity than you realize. The world around you strongly affects your mood, and there is no better example of that than how everything surrounding you influences your ultimate actions and outcomes.

Take some examples that are from your everyday life. Don't you just feel better in general when your bedroom and kitchen are completely clean? It is much more inviting to prepare a nice, healthy meal in a clean bright kitchen that has sunlight pouring in and a pleasing color scheme than a dark, dirty one with dishes piled up and napkins everywhere.

Taking control of your work environment is an important step towards living a productive life, but the ways to do so are going to be different, depending on whether you work at home or work in a company office.

If you work at home

- Set a place that is devoted just to getting work done. While it can be really tempting to work on your favorite couch while watching Netflix, it's sadly counterproductive. Having a spot where all you do is work means every time you sit down and work there you're associating it with work and will focus much quicker and get a lot more done.

- Get outside now and then! Staying inside and working two feet from your refrigerator is really nice, it's true. Sometimes, though, you can find yourself with cabin fever and the days all blend together in a weird haze. Having a favorite coffee shop or library where you can work, is a great way to switch up and experiment with a different work environment, which could surprisingly turn out more work friendly.

- Dress like you're actually working. It isn't just the environment itself you have to control. The most direct environment there is, can be your outfit. Wearing something that you would wear into an office puts you into a more professional mindset than working while dressed in flannel pajamas. There's nothing wrong with the occasional lazy day, but you should try and look presentable, as it will help your mindset and productivity, even if no one but you can actually see what you have on.

If you work in an office

- Invest in a quality pair of headphones. There is nothing more distracting than the constant noise of an office –

ringing phones, coworker conversations, fax machines, it can all be too much, especially considering the trend of open offices. Controlling the noise level you hear while focusing on work helps you control your productivity and life.

- Get some form of visual privacy. Whether it's a privacy screen, a barrier, or moving to an actual office, making sure you have control over your work environment and some degree of autonomy/privacy is crucial to productivity. Nobody is productive when they have other people looking over their shoulder all the time.

- Leave occasionally. Sitting inside under fluorescent lights isn't just bad for your skin and health, it is horrible for productivity. If you can't actually change the lighting around you, sit near a window or walk outside now and then.

- Keep your desk clear! While a lot of people will pile up lots of folders on their desk to look busy and avoid having to do more work, this isn't what someone who wants to be productive does. A cluttered desk represents a cluttered mind, and a cluttered mind is opposite to a productive and focused person.

Day 7: Being Your Own Boss

The best way to be a productive person is to work towards something that truly makes you excited. I know the common line is to work for something that makes you happy, but happiness can be fleeting. A box of chocolates makes you happy. A movie makes you happy.

What you want to be is not just happy, but excited. Fired up. Raring to go.

Some people find that feeling in jobs they love and are passionate about, and that's great. Usually those people are in the small minority though. The 9-5 workday can be comprised mostly of repetitive mundane tasks.

Being productive is easy when there's a really tangible reward that you have some control over. This is not the case with the vast majority of jobs for two main reasons.

The first of these reasons is that in many jobs there is no incentive to be more productive. Most employees know very well that doing work just leads to... more work. Employees are smart, and have no reason to break their backs if there isn't recognition coming.

The other reason is that when you're working to further someone else's agenda, it's hard to put your heart and soul in it. Being really in the zone and productive requires a certain passion and discipline that's hard to inspire in someone who is doing something they are unhappy with, as is the case with over 1/3 of surveyed employees in 2017.

Working for yourself can be a great way to reach higher productivity, focus, self-discipline, and success. If you don't want to be the boss of a company, where you have a lot of autonomy over what you do every day and how you do it, then working for yourself might be a good alternative. For a lot of people that kind of control over doing something they love in a pleasing environment, is as good if not better than being in control of their own company.

Others however, will struggle with finding true happiness out of productivity until it's time to take off life's training wheels and become their own boss. Being the boss of your own workplace leads you to be the boss of your own life. The confidence, drive, discipline, focus, and productivity you learn while branching out on your own simply cannot be replicated anywhere else.

CONCLUSION

Thank you for making it through to the end of *Self-Discipline: A 21 Day Step by Step Guide to Creating a Life Long Habit of Self-Discipline, Powerful Focus, and Extraordinary Productivity*. Let's hope it was informative and able to provide you with all of the tools you need to achieve your goals.

The next step is to take massive action on everything you have learned throughout this book. Take a good look at where you can apply these steps in your own life. It's so easy to read books like this and ride that high while never actually putting the principles into effect.

Finally, if you found this book useful in anyway, a review is always appreciated!

Printed in Great Britain
by Amazon